The Rugby Book For Kids, in paperback, first published in United Kingdom in 2024 by Rugby Books 4 Kids and printed by Amazon.

www.RugbyBooks4Kids.com

 @RugbyBooksForKids　　 @RugbyBooks4Kids　　 @RugbyBooksForKids

Original concept by Kurt Won.

This edition published in 2024.

From the Creator of My First Rugby Book

WRITTEN & ILLUSTRATED BY KURT WON

This book is dedicated to all the future rugby players
around the world.

The referee shouts **"ADVANTAGE"** when a team makes a mistake.
The whistle is blown if a scoring opportunity isn't something the opposing team can create.

Aa

Assistant Referee

Two assistant refs patrol the sidelines of the field.
The TMO sits outside the stadium in a van on wheels.

Accountability

Accountability means doing what you say you're going to do.
Whether that's practising your passing, catching or your kicking too.
It's a good idea to make a list of goals you want to pursue.
Put the list up. Cross off what's been done and celebrate with a woohoo!

Attitude

Attitude is everything, it controls how you think.
A bad attitude, like being a sore-loser, does really stink.
So learn to be humble and positive too.
Most importantly have an attitude that's can do.

All Blacks

The All Blacks are from New Zealand. They made running rugby their brand.
Silver ferns adorn their jersey and they are passionately followed by their supporters in the stands.

The Haka is their cultural dance that challenges their opponents.
The opportunity to face a haka is always a bonus.

Bb

Balls

Rugby balls were first made of leather.
They got very heavy when used in wet weather.
Now they make rugby balls from rubber
that make balls bounce more when kicking a grubber.

Bonus Point

A bonus point is awarded to teams who score
four tries or more. A team also get a bonus point for
losing by seven points or less.
Bonus points can make climbing the league
table a tight contest.

Box Kick

Box kicks are made from the base of a ruck or scrum.
The scrumhalf has to make sure he doesn't kick the ball
into his teammate's bum.

British Lions

The British and Irish Lions are a combined team.
For players from England, Scotland, Ireland and Wales,
playing for this team is a dream.

They tour every four years. Playing either South Africa,
Australia or New Zealand, their most fearsome peers.

Black Ferns

The national women's rugby team from
New Zealand is called the Black Ferns.

Don't give them space out wide because
they've got a lot of pace to burn.

They hold the most Rugby World Cup titles of any men's or
women's team. Facing or participating in their haka is every
rugby girl's dream.

Centres

There are two centres in a rugby team.
The inside centre wears number 12 and the outside 13.

They need to pass well and punch holes in defensive walls. Often you'll hear the wings shouting at them: "Pass me the ball!"

Cc

Concussion

Concussions happen when you get a knock to the head. You won't be allowed to continue playing until you've been HIA tested.

If you feel like you've been hit by a bus, take a seat, you may be concussed.

Composure

Staying calm when the pressure is high can be a struggle,
but it's a trait that all the best players must have when they have
big moments to juggle.

Making decisions under pressure is not easy.
So when things get tough take three deep breathes in,
nice and easy.

Remember this...
When emotions go high, intelligence goes low.
Practise the situations through simulations
so your composure can grow.

Conversion Kick

A chance for extra points after a try is scored.
Kick the conversion over and you have 2 points more.

As the kicker, practise your kicking routine continuously.
A defender can run and charge down your kick if timed correctly.

Dangerous Tackle

Tackles above the shoulders are too high.
Make a reckless tackle to the head and
the referee will send you off...good bye!

Deadball Line

The dead-ball line is the last line behind the posts.
Here you'll see supporters in the stand offering try scorers
a celebratory toast.

Dd

Drop Goal

Drop goals can take place from anywhere.
Try for 3 points from the halfway line, if you dare.

England

Rugby was started in England in 1823,
so we've been told.
The men's and women's teams together
have won three World Cup golds.

Ee

Energy

Positive energy starts with how you think.
If your opposition scores don't let your
energy sink.

Instead of dwelling on misfortune,
give the situation a different spin.
Remember, the team with the highest
energy generally wins!

#8 Eight

Tackles, crash balls, and stealing the ball off the floor.
The perfect number 8 can do all that and more.

Free Kick

A free kick is awarded for certain lesser offences. You can't kick for points but you you can trick less organised defences.

Take a quick tap, if your captain gives you the call or kick your wings a high ball.

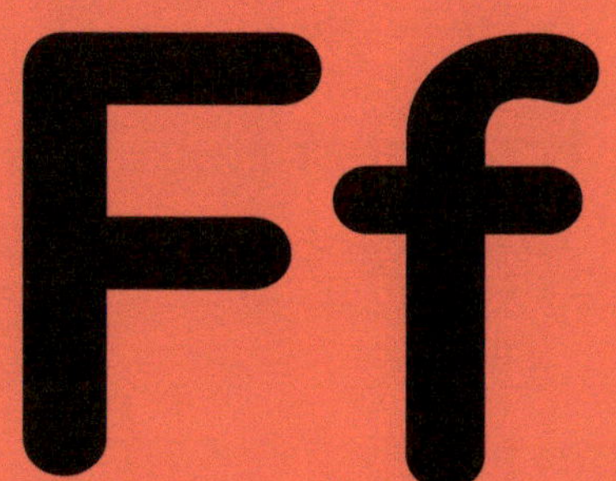

Flankers

Flankers wear the number 6 or 7. Called the blindside and openside, they're a match made in heaven.

Fullback

The fullback plays in the number 15 jersey.
Being able to kick with both feet is key.

They are the last line of defence and must be good
under the high ball. They're not usually players you'll
find in a brawl.

Flyhalf

The fly-half is the backline's play-maker.
Wearing the number 10, they're usually the
team's place-kicker.

Forward Pass

In rugby, backwards is the direction in which we pass.
The referees are helped by lines on the grass.

Goal Posts

The goal posts extend at least 3.4 metres into the sky.
Some have flags on top to help the goal kicker see if
there's a wind gusting by.

Posts are wrapped by cushions to protect players.
Cushions made of sponge in multiple layers.

Gg

Goal Kicker

Anyone can be a goal kicker.
Practise a lot and kick the points, and you may get a "Player of the Match"
sticker.

Gum Guard

Also known as a mouthguard, it helps to protect your teeth, jaws and skull.

They come in different colours, so choose a colour you like and break out of your shell.

Goal Line

Dot the ball down over the opposition goal line and you'll be awarded a try. Score more than fifty times and you'll be part of a special group of alumni.

Goals

The sky is the limit so set your goals high.
Setting goals will help your success fly.

Big goals can seem daunting.
So break them down into smaller goals.
Be humble when achieving them and not flaunting.

Half Time

Half time is blown usually when the time on the clock hits 40 minutes.

Teams take a ten minute break, talk about strategy and pushing past their limits.

Hooker

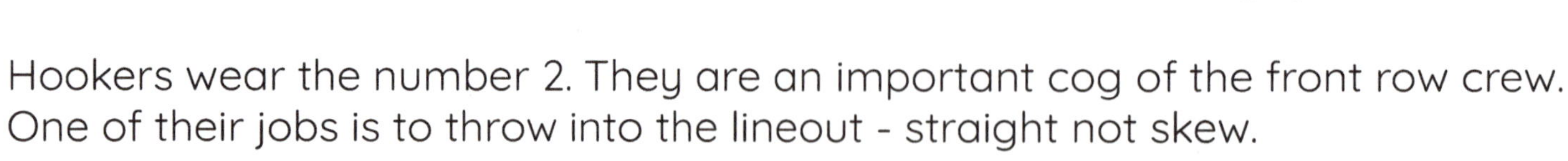

Hookers wear the number 2. They are an important cog of the front row crew. One of their jobs is to throw into the lineout - straight not skew.

High Five

Every time a teammate does something good, give them a high five.
It will raise your team's energy and spread a positive vibe.

High Tackle

High tackles are a no-no.
So keep tackles from the belly button
and below.

Head Injury Assessment (HIA)

If you get a knock to the head, the doctor may ask to do an HIA.
If they find you're concussed, then unfortunately you'll go off the field, M.I.A.

Ii

Inside Centre

Inside centres play with the number 12 on their back.

They have to be good at tackling, passing and making solid defences crack on attack.

Interception

Interceptions take great skill and timing. A run-away try for your team can be truly inspiring.

Make sure you don't slap the ball down.
You may cost your team a penalty and possibly, the championship crown.

Injury

Injuries are part of the game. Getting hurt is a real shame.
But keep your head high and with the right support
you'll be back soon to score a try.

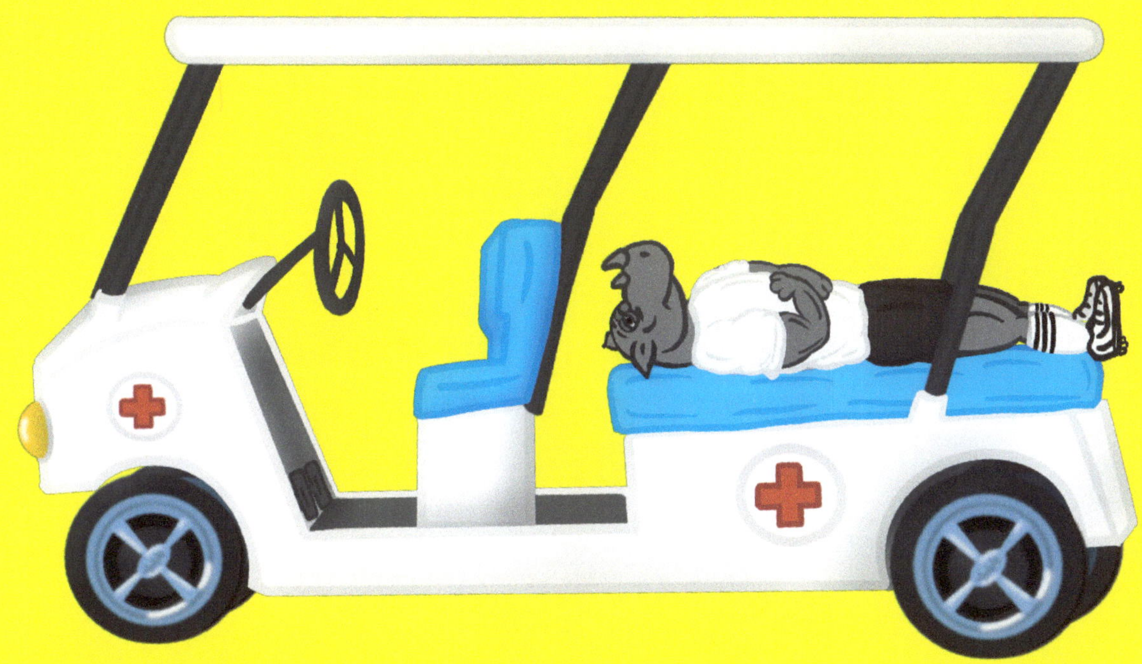

Inspiration

Surround yourself with people who are inspiring.
Mentors, coaches and fellow players can get your spirit firing.

Jumper

Locks are usually the main jumpers in a lineout.
Make sure not to take the jumpers legs out.

Jj

Junior & Minis Rugby

Junior rugby is where it all starts.
From 4 years and up, kids play with a big heart.

Coaches teach you how to catch and pass.
They'll have you playing fun games while training
on the grass.

Jerseys

Teams have two different colour jerseys - Home or Away.
One that is light and one that is dark, depending at which stadium they play.

Jackler

They're the first defender to get over the ball when an attacker is tackled down.

They can compete for the ball as long as their hands weren't first down on the ground.

Knock On

When you drop the ball forward, it's called a knock on.

"Advantage" is called if the opposition play on.

Kk

Kick Off

Before kick off, the captains gather to do a coin toss.
The winner chooses to kick or receive, but remember the referee
is always the boss.

BE
Kind

Kindness is an important part of the game.
Being a nice person brings no shame.

Kindness can mean a smile, or a helping hand.
A kind rugby player wins the hearts of all the fans.

Locks

Locks are lineout jumpers and lifted high to catch the ball.
They wear the number 4 and 5 and are very, very tall.

Lineout

In lineouts, teams stand one metre apart.
After a ball is kicked out, this is how the game restarts.

Loosehead Props

Loose-head props help lift jumpers in the lineout and are specialists in the scrum.

They're big, and muscular and wear jersey number one.

Low Tackle

Stop attackers in their tracks by tackling them low.

Tackle them around the ankles and there's nowhere they can go.

M

Match Day XV

Each side names a match day fifteen.
Win the game by choosing your dream team.

Match Officials

There are three officials on the field.
Two assistants with flags and one referee with a red card concealed.

m

Maul

A maul is formed when the ball is held up off the ground.

Once the ref calls "MAUL" theres no need for the defender to roll away if the mail goes down.

Medic

The medic and physio are an important part of the team.

They strap you up, stretch you out and make sure cuts are kept clean.

Mindset

Success in rugby isn't all about the pace and muscles.
It's more about winning your daily mental tussles.

Think positively and reprogram your mind to banish all negativity.

Nn

Neck Roll

A neck roll is a dangerous play.
Should you do it? No way!

Never Give Up

Some things we try end up in failure.
That doesn't mean that life will end in disaster.

Every failure is nothing but a test.
Try again and never give up, and show up doing your best.

No Try

The TMO has a lot of power watching his TV replay.
They check for knock-ons, forward passes or any illegal plays.

Their decision via radio, tells the referee if it's a try - Yay or Nay.

If the ball is not grounded over the line,
the ref will signal "Held Up" with a shout.

Play restarts with a goal line drop out.

Outside Centre

Outside centres wear the number 13.
A centre who passes to their wings is a
coaches dream.

Openside Flanker

The openside flanker wears the number 7.
Some are even fast enough to beat a wing
in jersey number 11.

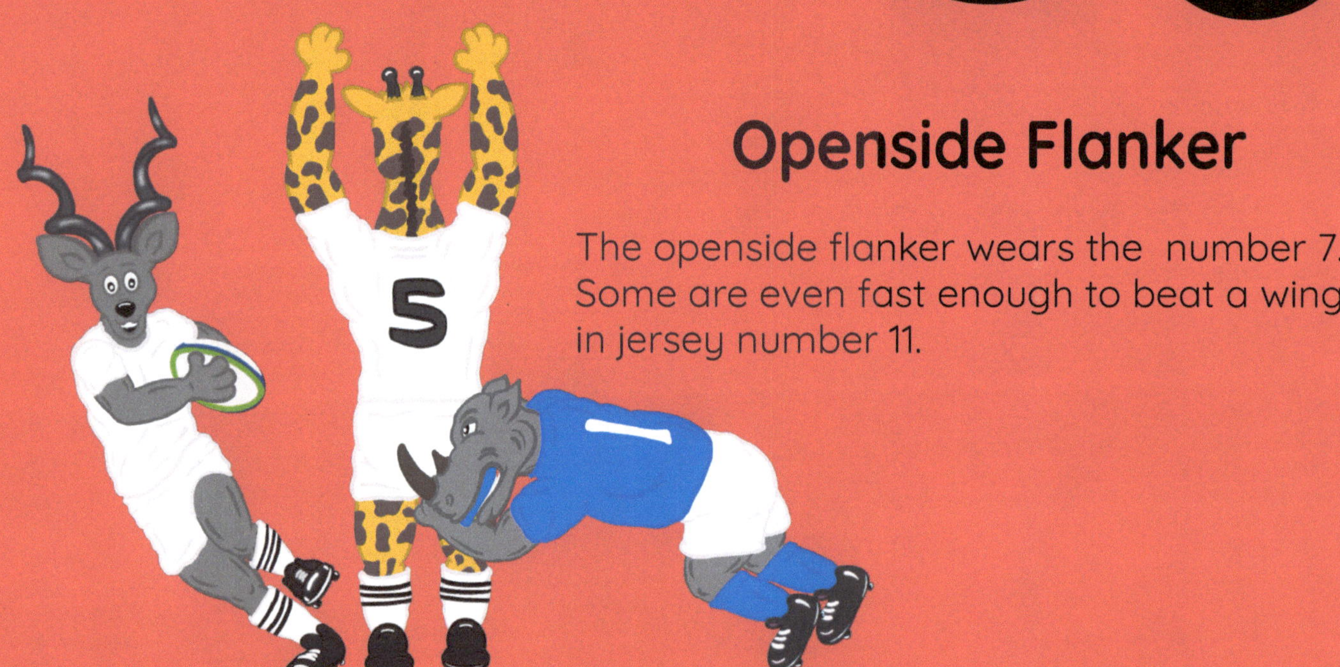

Obstruction

Acting as a shield to block a defender tackling your teammate is not allowed.
If this happens, even by mistake, the ref will blow their whistle out loud.

On-Side

Start behind the last foot of a ruck before you move forward to tackle will mean you're on-side.

If the ref shouts "Take a Step Back!" you must abide.

Offside Line

The offside line is an imaginary line.

It's formed by the last feet of the defence at the ruck.

All defenders must retreat behind and start their defensive movements from here at all times.

Offside

In the eyes of the referee you are committing a rugby crime if you're too lazy to get back behind the offside line.

Props

Props wear the numbers 1 or 3.
There's the loosehead and tighthead, respectively.

Pp

Positivity

Positivity is thinking that good things will come.
Setbacks and failures are normal so don't dwell on what can't be undone.

Penalty

A penalty is given when you break one of rugby's many laws.

Give away too many penalties and your coach will ask you to correct your flaws.

Pumas

The Pumas are the national team of Argentina.

They wear light blue and white and their supporters are passionate believers.

Passing

A rugby pass can come in many forms.
A pop pass, skip pass and torpedo pass are all part of match-day norms.

The most important thing is that the pass goes backwards, not forwards.

Quick Tap

Quick taps are taken from a free kick or penalty.
Take it from the mark or be called back by the referee.

Quick Thinking

Quick thinking requires being present to the game situation.
A good decision may result in a try against the opposition.

Questions

There's no such thing as a stupid question.
Questions unlock knowledge and help with your rugby progression.

So if you're confused about something, ask questions to get clarity in your mind. If someone asks a question that seems simple, remember to answer in kind.

Rugby

Rugby is played in 21 countries around the world by 8.5 million men, women, boys and girls.

It's a game of physical toughness, deftness and speed.
Also played by people with big hearts who do good deeds.

Rr

Respect

Treating others kindly, listening to them, and not hurting them is showing respect.

Accepting their decisions with no backchat is what referees expect.

Referee

Referees make sure players follow the rules.
They blow their whistle when players lose their cool.

Replacements

Replacements are substitutes who sit on the bench.
There are seven of them still fresh from stench.

If a player gets injured or has played their part, the substitute
will replace them and can give a tiring team a kick-start.

Red Roses

The Red Roses are the number one ranked
women's team in the world.

As England's womens team, they have one
of the best defenes that leaves opposition well tackled.

Scrum

After a skew lineout throw, a scrum resets play.
The referee will also call a scrum when a pass goes astray.

Ss

Scrumhalf

The scrumhalf wears the number nine.
Referees think they talk too much most of the time.

After feeding the ball into the scrum, if they want the ball,
they tap the number eight on the bum.

The scrumhalf is the link between the forwards and backline.
The fastest scrummies snipe around the ruck and down the touchline.

Springboks

After winning their fourth world cup, the Springboks got a massive standing ovation.
They are the pride of South Africa, the Green and Gold nation.

They are known for their rolling mauls that can travel great distances. Their huge forwards can crack open the toughest defences.

Sin Bin

The sin bin is a naughty chair for players who get a yellow card.

They wait for ten minutes hoping the opposition don't add any points to their scorecard.

Six Nations

The 6 Nations is an annual tournament, played between six teams in the Northern Hemisphere.

The rivalry between Ireland, England, Italy, France, Scotland and Wales is an intense affair.

Tt

Tackles

Good tackles stop an attacking team's flow.
They're best kept low, that means from the sternum and below.

Touchline

The touchline runs down both lengths of the field.

Kick the ball over this line when the clock turns red, and that's the match sealed.

Try

Scoring a try is every team's goal. Tries are worth 5 points and get the crowd dancing to rock n roll.

Defences better watch out for the speedy number eleven, because with a conversion, the try is now worth seven.

TMO (Television Match Official)

The television match official is also called the TMO.
They're often asked by the referee: "Try - Yes or No?"

22m Line

Twenty two metres from the goal line is the 22-metre line.

As the attacking team this area is where you want to spend most of your time.

Tag Rugby

Tag rugby is a non-contact game.

Stop a runner by grabbing their tag, but if you miss, there 's no shame.

Uu

Union

Rugby union is the game we play.

Players of other contact sports often migrate our way.

Up and Under

Gary Owens are high kicks to try force the opposing team into a blunder.
Most players just call it an up and under.

Vv

Versus

Playing styles between teams can be so diverse.

They may even come from a different rugby universe.

VS

Varsity Rugby

Rugby played at university is also called Varsity rugby.
There are many inter-university matches like the Oxford versus Cambridge derby.

Water Carriers

Water carriers keep the players hydrated and are an important part of the team.

They also offer tips to keep players focused like a laser beam.

Ww

Wallabies

The Wallabies from Down Under speak with a strong Australian twang.

They've won 2 World Cups and can surprise teams like a sneaky boomerang.

Wings

Wings wear the number 11 or 14.
The best wingers can sidestep a whole opposing team.

World Champions

The USA won the first women's world cup in 1991.
England got revenge at the next edition, the first half, battled under the sun.

But the Black Ferns from New Zealand, with six titles, will try
their best to extend their world cup trophy winning run.

The first mens World Cup was won by New Zealand in 1987.
The Springboks first try in a world cup final was scored by a
speedy number eleven.

There's been nine world cups split between champions of which
there are four. Being a world champion is every rugby player's
dream for sure.

X-Factor

A player with the X-Factor creates opportunities with a spark. Their side-steps and moves can get fans screaming with excitement across the park.

X-Ray

A bad injury will ruin your day.
Check for broken bones with an x-ray.

Yy

Yellow Card

Yellow cards are for repeated offences or dangerous plays.
Two yellow cards can get you banned for fourteen days.

Zz

Zero Tolerance
to Bullying

Rugby is a game for all shapes and sizes, big or small.
No matter your background, there's a place for one and all.

Referee Signals

Here are some of the signals and gestures you may see from a referee during a rugby match.

Playing Positions

1.
Loosehead
Prop

2.
Hooker

3.
Tighthead
Prop

4.
Lock

5.
Lock

6.
Blindside
Flank

7.
Openside
Flank

8.
Number
8

9.
Scrumhalf

10.
Flyhalf

11.
Left Wing

12.
Inside
Centre

13.
Outside
Centre

14.
Right Wing

15.
Fullback

Coach wants to test your RUGBY BRAIN

1. Your team is losing by 17 points. How many converted tries do you need to score to take the lead?

____

2. What are the 5 ways you can score points in a rugby match?

_______________   _______________

_______________   _______________   _______________

3. Which player holds the record for most tries scored in a single Rugby World Cup tournament?

____

4. Your teammate makes a mistake that allows the other team to score the match winning try. Your teammate feels really bad. What can you say or do to help them feel better?

____

____

Answers: 1. 3 (Three converted tries equals 21 points).
2. Try (5 pts), Conversion (2 points), Drop Goal (3 pts), Penalty kick (3 pts), Penalty Try (7 pts)
3. Portia Woodman-Wickliffe. She scored 13 tries for New Zealand in the 2017 Women's Rugby World Cup.
4. Here are some suggestions: Tell them it's ok and they can make up for it in the next game. Everyone makes mistakes. Give them a pat on the back with words of encouragement.

Crossword Puzzle

Down

2. Head contact may result in this injury
3. Number of points for a penalty try
4. Throws the ball into the lineout
5. They play in jerseys #6 or #7
6. Feeds the ball into the scrum

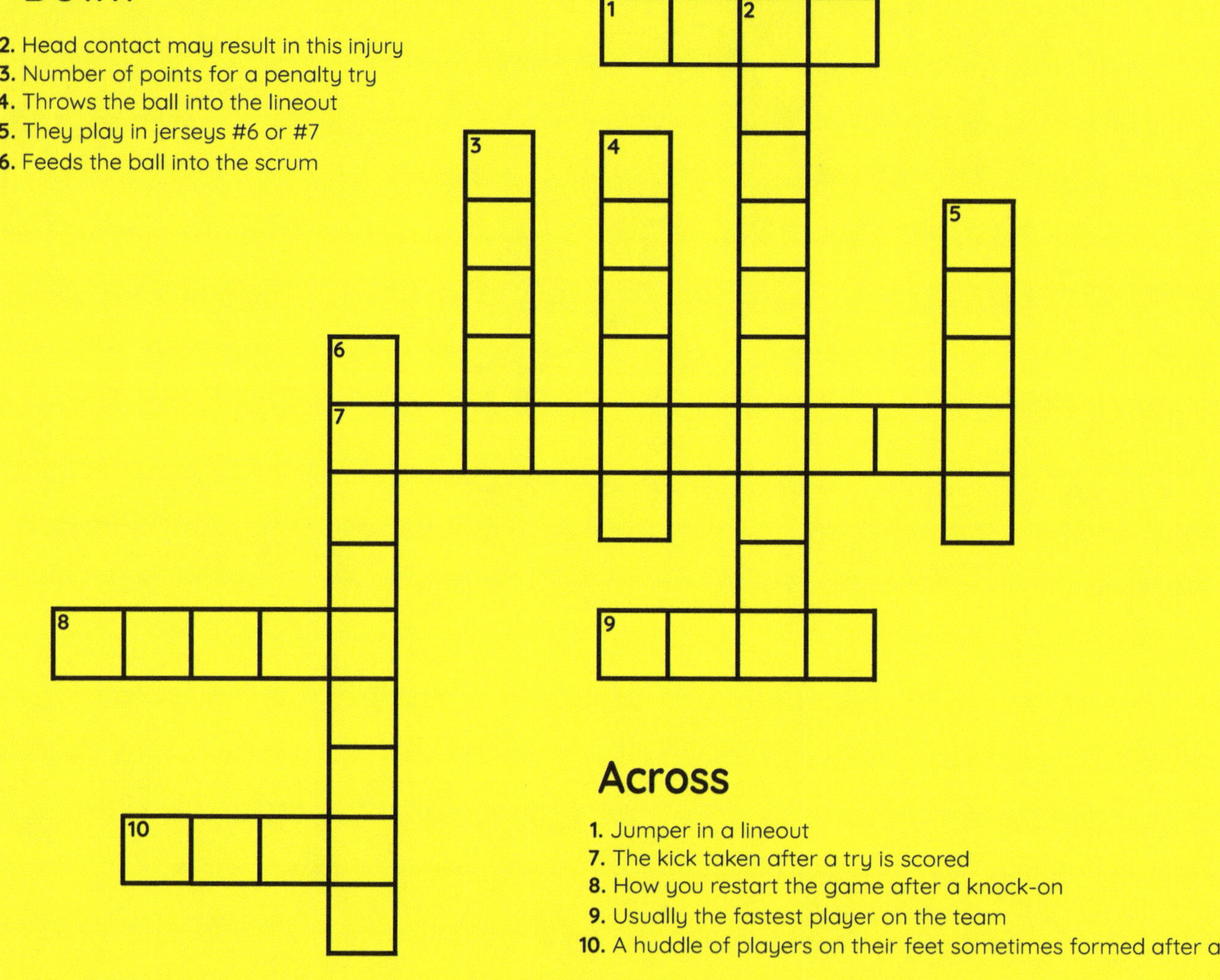

Across

1. Jumper in a lineout
7. The kick taken after a try is scored
8. How you restart the game after a knock-on
9. Usually the fastest player on the team
10. A huddle of players on their feet sometimes formed after a lineout

Autographs

Use this page to collect autographs from your favourite players.

Player Name **Number #** **Autograph**

Useful Links

 https://www.englandrugby.com/play

 https://community.wru.wales

 https://www.irishrugby.ie/playing-the-game

 https://scottishrugby.org/clubs-and-schools/ways-to-play

 https://usa.rugby/youth-and-high-school

 https://rugbycanada.sportlomo.com

 https://ferugby.es/plataforma-de-registro-get-into-rugby

 https://www.hkrugby.com/play-rugby

 https://rugby.nl/rugby/beginnen-met-rugby

 https://mexrugby.com/el-rugby/get-into-rugby

Create a Customised Rugby Book for your Club!

Rugby Books For Kids provides grassroots and professional rugby clubs the opportunity to create bespoke, customised rugby books to help **educate**, **inspire** and **engage** rugby-loving children.

Customise the kit of the characters, add pages to promote your club and create an immersive experience for players and parents.

Contact us below for more information

Follow us on social media and post a photo of you with this book for a chance to be featured!

 **@RugbyBooksForKids**    **@RugbyBooks4Kids**    **@RugbyBooksForKids**

Other books in this series:

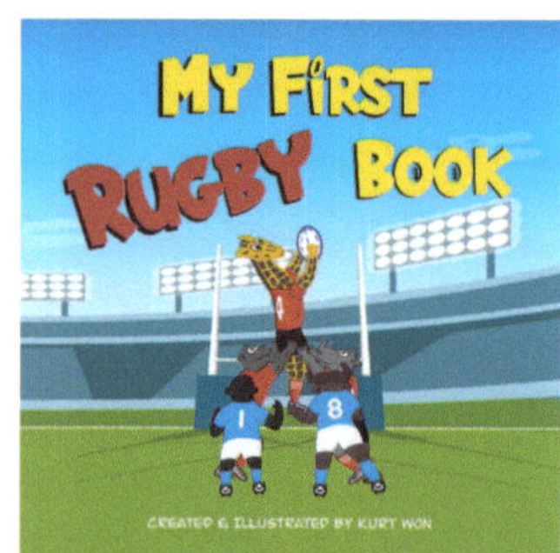

Suitable for children under 7 years old